# SENEY
## NATIONAL WILDLIFE REFUGE
# *Its Story*

Elizabeth Browne Losey

*Typical Seney Landscape*

E. LOSEY

©2003 Elizabeth Browne Losey

ISBN  0-9727834-0-7
Library of Congress Control Number:  2002096950

Published by Elizabeth Browne Losey

Printed in the United States of America
by Lake Superior Press, Marquette, Michigan 49855

First Edition 2003
10  9  8  7  6  5  4  3  2  1

Cover Photograph by Elizabeth Browne Losey

# Dedication

C. S. Johnson and Duke

# Clarence S. Johnson

*First Refuge Manager of*
*Seney National Wildlife Refuge*

# FOREWORD

Elizabeth Losey has produced a small volume of information about Seney National Wildlife Refuge that is a treasure. It is not just a guide to this remarkable refuge and the marvelous places and creatures it harbors; it is an insight to the creation and management of such a place. It reports what it took to establish this refuge many years ago, and offers an idea of the challenges the men and women who are responsible for such places actually face, as it describes what is to be seen and enjoyed as a result.

Mrs. Losey is a rare creature in her own right: she was hired as a young biologist—by the revered visionary responsible for creating the early National Wildlife Refuge System, J. Clark Salyer—in the early days of his long tenure. Her experience gives unusual credibility to her observations about this refuge. Moreover, her interest over the years has included going back to the original documents that describe happenings on the refuge, so her reporting is based on records made by the people who experienced the evolution of this place, day after day.

Elizabeth Losey makes us aware of small things that affected Seney, as well as the sometimes startling events that make any refuge employee's life one that is rarely free of excitement and challenge.

I remember vividly the excitement that arose from the famed "Seney fire" in the early 1970's; I cannot possibly imagine the range of feelings that must have run through the first refuge manager's mind when he was made custodian of a Conscientious Objectors' Camp early in World War II – and of the less-than-cooperative residents of this facility. I do know that what Elizabeth Losey has to tell us about Seney National Wildlife Refuge is factual, fascinating, and told by a person who has spent a lifetime in love with this bit of America's natural heritage.

I commend this book to you. It is, as the vernacular has it, the "real stuff" about people who have had the "right stuff," and about the splendid national treasure they look after for you.

Lynn A. Greenwalt
Former Director (1973-1981)
U.S. Fish and Wildlife Service

*Young Bobcat*                                                    R. DENOMME

# INTRODUCTION

*A* small island in Florida's Indian River was the traditional nesting site for hundreds of pelicans, egrets, ibises and roseate spoonbills - all vulnerable to the ruthless yearly slaughter by plume hunters answering the insatiable demands of the millinery trade which required bird feathers for decorating women's hats. To stop this indiscriminate killing, President Theodore Roosevelt by Executive Order created Pelican Island Bird Sanctuary in 1903. The establishment of this

*Black Bear*                          K. SOMMERER

Refuge was the first step in our national policy of providing protection for our country's wildlife resources. It was also the beginning of the National Fish and Wildlife Refuge system, which now, 100 years later, has grown to include more than 500 refuges and 93,000,000 acres.

The Seney National Wildlife Refuge ranks 82nd among the refuges according to date of establishment. Its 95,238 acres makes it the eighth largest refuge east of the Mississippi River.

*Coyotes Howling*                              R. DENOMME

Saw-whet Owl                    R. BAETSEN

The Seney Refuge has always been a mecca for people wishing to experience its varied and prolific wildlife. Over 211 species of birds including the majestic Bald Eagle, Trumpeter Swans, Sandhill Cranes, Canada Geese, ducks, loons, a wide variety of song birds and even the elusive Yellow Rail can sometimes be seen. In addition to the usual mammals such as deer, muskrat and mink, in very recent years, a few wolves

Pileated                    R. BAETSEN
Woodpecker

and moose as well as pine martin and fisher have moved into the area affording the exciting and rare possibility of glimpsing them. Seney's rich and varied landscape of marshes, pine-covered knolls and pools has lured both amateur and professional photographers to capture its beauty and appeal on film. Roads and nature walks provide convenient access to a large portion of the Refuge.

Pine Martin                    R. BAETSEN

The story of the Seney National Wildlife Refuge is an account of the transformation of a large tract of wild land that had been misused by man's efforts into an area fulfilling its inherent natural capabilities. The collapse of a giant land speculation scheme made possible the establishment of the Seney Refuge.

Ruffed Grouse Displaying          R. BAETSEN

Ruffed Grouse Drumming          R. BAETSEN

*Sedge Marsh and Red Pine*                                                    USFWS

# THE SENEY MARSHES

*T*he large tract of land known as the Seney marshes occupies an extensive area in the northwestern section of Schoolcraft County in the central part of the Upper Peninsula of Michigan. These vast open marshes of dense sedge, willow and alder stretch for miles in all directions broken only by slightly elevated sandy knolls and ridges supporting vigorous stands of red, white and jack pine trees. Five rivers or creeks flow roughly in a northwest to southeast direction through the area. The western part of the tract is characterized by a series of string bogs, a unique biological formation. These string bogs, now accorded recognition as a Registered National Natural Landmark, are known as the Strangmoor Bog and are located in a 25,000-acre Wilderness

*Strangmoor Bog*                                                              USFWS

Area. They are a unique land formation and are one of the most southern sub-arctic patterned bogs still in existence in North America. As the last great glacial ice sheet receded, the combined action of wind and water piled the exposed sand into long parallel dunes, which are now covered with red and white pine, white birch, and aspen. Between each of the dunes are low lying areas of wetlands supporting plants such as bog birch, leatherleaf, pitcher plant, bog rosemary and sphagnum moss.

*Aerial View of South End*  E. LOSEY

*Gray's Creek*  E. LOSEY

The marsh was home to deer, muskrats, mink and beaver. Sandhill Cranes nested undisturbed. Waterfowl, however, were largely absent since the rank sedge growth of the marshes was much too dense and dry to attract them. The pine-bearing knolls were soon logged off wherever economically feasible. As might be expected, fire uncontrolled and unchecked burned over high ridges and marshes many times. Such were the Seney marshes at the beginning of the 20th century.

*Driggs River*  E. LOSEY

*Walsh Ditch*

# WESTERN LAND SURETY COMPANY DEVELOPMENT

*A*round 1908 a land syndicate called the Western Land Surety Company bought from the Cleveland Cliffs Mining Company the Seney marshes as an investment. They planned to drain the area and promote it as prime agricultural land. The company paid approximately one dollar per acre and began their development program chiefly by digging several drainage ditches in the marsh. One such ditch, the Walsh Ditch, is sixteen miles long. It commences in the north at highway M-28 and eventually drains south into the Manistique River. It was dug at a cost of approximately nine cents a yard for removing the soil.

Lured by extravagant propaganda, high pressure publicity, and by elaborate plans for the town of New Seney, but most of all by the alluring promise of the rich-looking black peat soil, farmers from all over the mid-west bought land (frequently sight unseen) to fulfill their dreams of establishing homesteads. Unfortunately, they soon found that the black fertile-looking peat was lying over a coarse porous sand base and as soon as the spring rains stopped, the newly planted crops quickly wilted and dried. Also the peat soil was very susceptible to frost. Once the marsh sedge cover was turned under by the plow, thus exposing the peat to the surface, it quickly dried out and the wind soon blew it off, leaving nothing but the base sand. So one by one the discouraged farmers gave up, abandoned their homestead holdings and moved away. Only old cellar holes and ditches are left to mark their futile attempts to force the land to do what it wasn't capable of doing. The land eventually reverted to the state for tax delinquency.

# GOVERNMENT ACQUISITION OF THE LAND

*J*n 1935 the U.S. Fish and Wildlife Service stepped in and acquired the Seney marshes from the State of Michigan. It was its belief that this abandoned land, idle and deserted, could be turned into something useful - the production of wildlife. The acquisition of the approximately 96,000 acres was not a simple matter. A major portion was accomplished by transfer of these tax delinquent reverted lands from the State of Michigan to the United States Fish and Wildlife Service. Some undeveloped holdings were acquired by direct purchase from the owners. The price averaged about two dollars per acre.

However, about one-quarter of the total acreage earmarked for the new Refuge had to be acquired through the exercise of "eminent domain," the legal power of the federal government to appropriate private property for public use in return for compensation. There were many owners who did not wish to sell their land, either because they thought the price offered was too low or because they simply did not wish to move from their property. However, when the Government invoked the right of "eminent domain," they had no choice. Three different groups totaling seventy-one individuals brought suit against the U.S. Government challenging its authority to confiscate their property. In all three cases the court found against the plaintiffs and in favor of the Government. The plaintiffs were forced to accept the verdict, relinquish their property and accept an average price of $1.80 per acre.

The justification for this action by the Government was set

*Smith Homestead*

E. LOSEY

forth as follows: "That it is necessary and advantageous for the United States to acquire title to the lands hereinafter described to carry out the Wild-Life Program of the Bureau of Biological Survey of the Department of Agriculture and the Seney Migratory Waterfowl Refuge Project which provides for the acquisition of the hereinafter described land for the conservation and development of water resources; reforestation; sanctuary for the nesting, resting and feeding of migratory waterfowl and other forms of wild life, in effectuation of the treaty between the United States and Great Britain, August 16, 1916, (39 Stat. 1702); recreational facilities, including hunting and wild life study."

*Chicago Farm*

These words express a noble and commendable objective, but bring cold comfort to a land-owner forced to give up all that he had accomplished through many years of his life creating a home out of tree-covered land - clearing, plowing and planting, setting out fruit trees, raising a barn for his horses and cattle and building a home to shelter his family.

The exercise of the right of "eminent domain" while accomplishing its objective of securing the land needed for the Seney National Wildlife Refuge, brought heartache and irreversible loss to some people. Today these old homestead clearings are empty and silent. All traces of human occupation have long vanished. The 400-acre Holbrook homestead was (and is today) known as the Chicago Farm because the Chicago Land and Lumber Company work horses were stabled there during the off-season of the company's logging operations. A few apple trees (which still after three-quarters of a century bear delicious fruit) are all that mark the location of the 160-acre Losey farm. For all the rest, the memory of their existence and location is still perpetuated to this day by the widely accepted habit of referring to these areas by the name of their long-ago owners such as the Dick Smith place, the Guy Chesebro farm, the Steve Stillson tract, the Bullock Ranch.

The 95,238 acres which comprise the Seney Refuge are not all marsh. There is a rich diversity of habitat types represented within its boundaries. Bottomland timber borders the rivers. Pine-covered sandy knolls and ridges are numerous. Northern leatherleaf bogs occur frequently. Maple, birch, and beech hardwoods are found in a wide zone bordering the Manistique and Driggs rivers and Pine Creek. Open sedge marshes and thick growth of cedar, tamarack, poplar, and spruce are characteristic of the western third of the Refuge. To the north there are extensive grasslands along with scattered groves of poplars. These were kept open by the countless wild fires that burned the peat soil right down to the underlying sand. This was excellent country for upland grouse such as Prairie Chicken and Sharp-tailed Grouse. However, with the suppression of fire, the open grassland rapidly closed in and reverted to willow brush and poplar growth that has greatly lessened its suitability for the upland grouse.

# C. S. JOHNSON - REFUGE MANAGER
## 1935 - 1949

inanced by duck stamp money and appropriations from Congress, aided by Civilian Conservation Corps (CCC) and Works Progress Administration crews and with the loyal efforts of the Refuge staff under the outstanding leadership of Refuge Manager C. S. Johnson, the U.S. Fish and Wildlife Service embarked on an extensive construction program designed basically to create areas of open water and to divert water from the ditches into the dry sedge marshes.

*CCC Crew* USFWS

The local CCC Camp was located just south of Germfask on the banks of the Manistique River. The young teenage recruits contributed an important and major share of the work required to build the Seney Refuge. They also won the hearts of the people of Germfask by their outstanding performance as baseball players. In the dreary economic days of the 1930's and 1940's baseball fever was high everywhere, especially in the small towns of the Upper Peninsula; it was the one free pastime everyone could enjoy. Germfask was no exception. As the local CCC team continued to triumph over its rivals, the quest for the regional championship became so heated that the camp administrator bent the eligibility rules to allow the recruitment of a fifteen-year Germfask lad because of his proven outstanding ability at playing short-stop.

## Building the Refuge

he task of building a refuge "from scratch" involved a great deal of preliminary engineering before actual construction could commence. Service roads had to be laid out following the natural ridges and knolls as much as possible. Eventually more than 100 miles of road were constructed. Ground elevations were required to determine the extent and location

*Aerial View of Refuge After Construction* USFWS

of each of the pools. This pool system depended on water diverted from Marsh Creek and several diversion and drainage ditches which run in a northwest to southeast direction through the Refuge. This diverted water flows from one pool to another below it following the natural drop in elevation. The areas to be flooded had to be cleared of all trees and brush. This produced thousands of cords of merchantable wood. Spillways, regulating the flow of water from one pool to another, were built of wooden stop-logs. Over succeeding years these wooden structures were gradually replaced with more permanent concrete ones. Bulldozers and draglines were required to construct the dikes impounding the water in each pool. Once built, these dikes had to be stabilized with tons of gravel and their banks protected from erosion with extensive plantings of grass and legumes. When the pool system was finally completed, it

*Felling White Pine*                    USFWS

*Logs Ready for Haulage by Horses*                    USFWS

*Hand Labor on
Bridge Construction*

comprised a total of 21
major impoundments with
7,000 surface water acres.

Along with the
development of the road
and pool systems, an active
building program was car-
ried on simultaneously to
provide the office head-
quarters, staff housing,
garage and maintenance

*Decking the Bridge*

*The Dragline at Work*

*Stacking the Logs*

Early Sand Dike without Gravel
Surface or Stabilized Bank

*Early Stage of*
*Bridge Building*

and repair shops required to meet the needs of the Refuge. As was to be expected when building a new refuge, many problems were encountered. One by one they were tackled and eventually solved, if not fully, at least partially.

*CCC Crew Off to Work*

*Pouring Concrete for Water Control Structure*

## Soil and Vegetation Improvement

One of the most important challenges was the lack of fertility of the Refuge soil. Basically it is either a coarse sand lacking in nutrients, or it is a peat soil which is notoriously difficult to handle. Largely because of this, there was a lack of desirable moist land plants of the type used by ducks for food and cover, such as bullrush, smartweed, and various pondweeds including *brasenia*. An aggressive program of planting emergent plants around the pool edges was undertaken and continued over a considerable period of time. These plantings not only provided duck food and some cover but also helped stabilize the dike bases by reducing erosion caused by wave action. In further efforts to overcome the lack of fertility in the pools, some fertilizing was done to encourage a more vigorous growth of aquatic food plants. Pools were drained, fertilized and then re-flooded. Gradually over the years since this practice was inaugurated, the aquatic vegetation has become established in increasing amounts so that now most pools have a very satisfactory growth of such desirable duck food plants as wild celery and many of the preferred pondweeds.

Frequent attempts to establish wild rice were unsuccessful. A total of more than 1,000 pounds of seed were used, but the heavy depredations on the young sprouts by muskrats, deer and geese prevented the plants from growing and producing seed. Only those plantings enclosed by fencing survived to mature. This was obviously not a feasible method to be done on a large scale.

*Planting Emergents*                    E. LOSEY

Another problem of major importance which continues to exist at the Refuge is the large acreage of thick willow and alder brush semi-dry marshes. This type of vegetation offers little to many forms of wildlife, especially waterfowl, although the deer do browse on the willow. There is not enough water in them, the vegetation is too rank and dense, and there are no open water areas present. Over the years various methods such as blasting, the use of herbicides, and burning have been tried to open up this type of marsh, but to-date none has been proved very successful in alleviating the condition.

# Forestry Practices

The approximately 30,000 acres of forest, roughly 33% of the entire Refuge, were from the very beginning recognized as a valuable asset. During the early days of developing the Refuge it was necessary to remove a considerable amount of timber both from the areas that were to be flooded and from the ridges and knolls along which the roads were to be built. This yielded a large number of cords of both pulpwood and saw logs.

Responding to a 1948 request from the Society of American Foresters to set aside certain tracts of virgin and natural forests that would be preserved in perpetuity in an unchanged condition, three of the Society's forest types were selected by Harvey Saunders, the Refuge forester, a seasoned and experienced logging camp boss and veteran timber cruiser from Maine. The areas chosen were as follows: Type 3 - 80 acres of virgin red pine; Type 10 - 50 acres of mature eastern white

*Harvey Saunders*　　　　　　　　　　　USFWS

pine and eastern hemlock; Type 12 - 320 acres of mixed mature sugar maple, American beech and yellow birch. These tracts designated to remain completely untouched by human activity and to be monitored on a regular basis, still stand today as Natural Areas.

*Checkerboard Clear Cutting*　　　　　　　USFWS

Many other forest-related activities were carried on in the early years of Refuge development. A considerable amount of mature pulpwood, principally jack pine and poplar was harvested to maintain a balance of age classifications and to improve game habitat. Most of the jack pine was fifty years or older. In 1949 it was estimated that there was yet to be cut over a period of years a minimum of 2,000,000 board feet of hardwoods and hemlock and 2,000,000 - 4,000,000 board feet of white and red pine. The removal of this mature timber was designed to perpetuate the forest by allowing young healthy stands of trees to become established, to provide suitable openings in the forest canopy, and to insure optimum conditions that would permit the growth of trees and shrubs required by wildlife for food and cover.

*Planting Trees at Driggs River Road*                    E. LOSEY

Planting of trees, especially red oak to provide acorns for food for wildlife such as deer and grouse, in the many natural clearings in the uplands was an important Refuge activity. For example, during the years 1947-1949, 1,200 red oak seedlings were planted in various suitable locations in the Refuge.

In the 1980's 22,884 acres of forest habitat were inventoried according to type and a plan developed to re-establish forest openings in certain areas that would enhance wildlife habitat. The use of selective cutting of trees as a tool for creating certain types of desired habitat was regularly utilized.

## Bird Banding

*A*n active banding program of ducks and geese was undertaken and is still carried on each fall. At first large walk-in trap enclosures were used. Eventually this was supplemented by rocket-propelled nets. Rounding up the Canada Geese during their flightless period by herding them into an enclosure so they could be banded was also done. In later years banding has been expanded to include mist netting of song birds.

*Waterfowl Banding*                    USFWS

# CPS 135 - Conscientious Objectors Camp

*J*n May of 1944 an event occurred which rudely jolted the Refuge out of its normal routine. This was the recommissioning of the CCC complex adjacent to the Refuge as CPS 135 camp. The camp was to be administered by Seney Refuge for forty conscientious objectors (i.e., men who refused to enlist in the Army for reasons of conscience). From May 12 when the first contingent of men arrived until May 31 of the following year when the camp was closed, the administrators were, in the words of Refuge Manager C. S. Johnson, "in turn bewildered, shocked and eventually quite permanently brought to the view of detestation for the average objector." These conscientious objectors deliberately and persistently sought to break up camp functions. They excelled in making life as miserable as possible for the supervisory personnel.

It soon became obvious that few of the men would work, that camp discipline could not be maintained, that men would readily resort to malingering, would go AWOL at will, destroy property, exhibit indecent exposure, commit assault and battery, fail to obey orders and openly scorn any loyalty whatsoever to the United States – the list was endless. All this was subject to no penalty. Desertion was the only offense for which there was any legal redress.

As Johnson wryly commented, "we were up to our necks in trouble with no hope in sight." The conscientious objectors frankly admitted that they fully understood the limitations of the regulations and the law governing them and they were well aware of just how far they could go without incurring penalties. Their goal was to make things just as intolerable as they possibly could and in this they

> *"We were up to our necks in trouble with no hope in sight."*
>
> — *C. S. Johnson*

were eminently successful. Eventually after 388 days the nightmare ended and the camp was closed. Some twenty-two objectors were sent to federal prisons, the rest were discharged for one reason or another, by far the majority for physical or mental unfitness.

In summing up the experience Johnson wrote that "It can be truthfully said that the main activity of the camp was refusal to work." To him the mere mention of the term "conscientious objector" opened old wounds which were long in healing. He concluded, "We hope now to forget the episode." C. S. Johnson's account of the entire 388-day conscientious objector experience as written in his masterful and colorful prose is well worth reproducing in its entirety. It is appended as Appendix III.

## Canada Goose Introduction

*A*n event of major significance occurred in late January 1936. On a blustery sub-zero day 300 Canada Geese arrived on the doorstep of the Refuge. These geese had been pinioned, that is rendered permanently incapable of flying by cutting a wing tendon. They were a gift from Henry Wallace who had been successfully raising Canada Geese for many years on his farm fifty miles southwest of Detroit.

From the very inception of the Refuge, it had been a cherished hope that Canada Geese could be introduced into the Upper Peninsula of Michigan by establishing a breeding population within the Refuge. These 300 geese were the first step toward the realization of this hope.

Near the Refuge subheadquarters a small two-acre holding pen containing a small water hole was quickly prepared to receive the birds and there they remained until spring. Soon thereafter, development of a 400-acre pasture by Gray's Creek was undertaken and eventually a fence was completed enclosing the 400 acres which included three pools impounded by dikes. Available natural foods were supplemented with a mixture of corn, barley and oats.

Gradually during the first ten years the number of pinioned birds steadily declined from the original 300. However, successful nesting not only within the enclosed goose pasture but also in other nearby suitable areas resulted in encouraging numbers of locally produced goslings.

*Spring Return of the Geese*

After six years (1942) the pinioned geese were hatching some 200 young annually. These birds, left full-wing, migrated south each year, but few of them returned to the Refuge in the spring. By 1945 only forty-five pinioned birds remained. That fall all of the approximately 900 free-flying geese that had spent the summer months within the Refuge departed on their migration south. The great question on everyone's mind "Will they return in the spring?" Early in March of 1946 this question was answered. The air resounded with loud honking as sixteen geese set their wings and landed in the Refuge pool. These were just the first of the many returning to the Refuge in increasing numbers each day. Their return was proof that a breeding population of Canada Geese at the Seney Refuge had been successfully achieved.

This successful outcome was not attained without the dedication and tireless efforts of C. S. Johnson and the entire Refuge staff. Constant 24-hour vigilance was required. In the very first year during the winter months, it was necessary to chop holes through the ice every day to provide water access for the geese. To deter coyotes and foxes from preying on the pinioned geese within the enclosure, lanterns were hung from trees. Once a plow crew had to battle from dusk to dawn a marsh fire which threatened to burn the goose enclosure. A major set-back occurred when spring floods washed out a section of the goose pen fence and eighty geese went floating down the Manistique River, swept away by the current, and because they were pinioned, were powerless to return to their penned enclosure.

By 1951 the need to provide additional grazing and feeding areas for the rapidly expanding Refuge goose flock was recognized. Accordingly, an extensive program of planting selected fields with cover crops of grain and legumes was begun. This was very successful and received heavy use by the geese. In addition during 1970 and 1971 two prescribed burns were successfully carried out designed to induce new growth of the succulent grasses utilized by geese and Sandhill Cranes.

The Canada Goose population, although securely established, was facing serious problems. For several years the number of geese returning to the Refuge each spring was steadily declining. For example, in 1966 only 450 - 500 birds returned. In addition the kill during the fall hunting season was an excessively high percentage of the resident birds. To correct this, commencing in 1966 a no-hunting zone was established on the northeast and south side of the Refuge. This relieved the hunting pressure on the local birds so that after four years, goose numbers had recovered sufficiently to permit the elimination of the closed area. However, it was understood that the closed zone was to be reactivated whenever the kill exceeded 500 birds.

*Canada Goose and Eggs*          C. HENRY

Another problem confronting the Seney geese was the devastating die-offs of large numbers of goslings. In 1960, 87% of the goslings died. In 1963 the mortality was 500. By 1964 it had climbed to 690, and in 1968 the tally was 1022, or 75% of the goslings. Four years later in 1972 the die-off was 76% of the goslings. The problem of gosling die-offs continued with alarming frequency. In 1977 there was an almost 100% gosling mortality. In 1974 the number of goose eggs hatched declined to 457. This marked a discouraging trend from the 800 average yearly hatch for the previous ten-year period 1963-1973.

As a result of long-term intensive studies on *leucocytozoon* and black flies, Dr. Barry Tarshis finally determined that a species of black fly (*Simulium innocens*) was the chief vector in infecting the goslings with *leucocytozoon* (*avian malaria*). When the hatching time of the black flies and of the goslings coincided, the die-off was catastrophic resulting in losses up to 80% of the year's production. The effect of the infection was quick, violent and massive. These die-offs appeared to occur about every four years.

The joint study on the drug *clopidae* to determine its possible

*Pinioned Geese During the Winter*          USFWS

effects on the parasite *leucocytozoon* was terminated when the results of the study showed that while the drug successfully eliminated the parasite from the blood stream, it did not from the body tissue. Therefore it was not useful for successful eradication of the parasite.

Nest predation was another factor that affected the health of the goose population. Some years it accounted for 44% of the nests. Crows were responsible for 63% of this loss. Coyotes, too, took their toll. In an effort to reduce nest predation, trapping was carried on to keep the coyote population at a reasonable level. In addition, water levels in the pools were raised each spring to facilitate early ice break-up, thus helping to safeguard island nesting sites from marauding coyotes.

*Canada Goose on Nest*                                          E. LOSEY

In the end, all the time, trouble and effort paid off. The Canada Goose was successfully established as a permanent resident of the Upper Peninsula. It enriched the wildlife of the area. By eventually providing a population numerous enough to offer hunting opportunities, it provided significant economic benefits to the local communities.

The effects of this successful establishment of the Canada Geese were reflected in the increasing popularity of goose hunting in the surrounding area. Local land owners quickly cashed in on the goose hunters and built goose blinds, in the words of Refuge Manager Cordia Henry, "some as large as the proverbial barn," and charged fees for hunting on their land as high as $25 for two guns per day and $20 per gun-day. It was feared that this "over commercialization" was a bit premature since, as of 1955, the Refuge flock was not sufficiently well established to permit such a heavy kill. By 1956, it was estimated that the Refuge population numbered approximately 3,000 wild free-flying geese composed of 540 adult nesting birds, 1,000 goslings and 1,500 non-breeding birds. None of the original 300 captive pinioned birds remained. Over the succeeding years the geese dispersed over a sufficiently wide area so that the local harvest of the Refuge flock has not been considered excessive.

After fourteen years of directing the construction and early development of the Seney Refuge, C. S. Johnson was transferred to the Upper Souris Refuge in North Dakota. On August 24, 1949, barely three months at his new post, he and his pilot were killed in an airplane crash during an aerial survey of farmers' fields to assess crop damage caused by waterfowl depredation. Johnson left an impressive legacy: the establishment of the 96,000 acre Seney Refuge on a firm foundation and the successful introduction of a resident Canada Goose population.

*Boundary Work Train and Crew*                                    C. HENRY

# CORDIA J. HENRY - REFUGE MANAGER
# 1949 - 1958

*J*ohnson's successor was Cordia J. Henry who served as Refuge Manager from 1949 - 1958. During his nine years, the Refuge infrastructure was improved as well as expanded. The access and dike roads were stabilized, upgraded and in some places even graveled. The old wooden stop-log water structures were replaced with modern iron controls and wooden bridges replaced with concrete ones. Banding of geese and ducks was a continuing activity. Other ongoing programs were the planting of aquatic vegetation and the removal of brush from small islands in the pools to provide nesting and roosting sites for the geese.

*Riverside Dike - Dragline at Work*                               USFWS

During Henry's administration two major projects were undertaken. The first was posting and fencing the entire 50-mile boundary line of the Refuge. The second was the construction of the four-mile Riverside Dike designed to form the 950-acre Marsh Creek impoundment in the southwest section of the Refuge. This is the largest in the Refuge pool system. Started in 1952, it was completed in 1957.

*Marsh Creek Pool Spillway Construction*　　　　USFWS

## Trapping

For many years trapping was an activity allowed on the Refuge. At various times, muskrat, mink, beaver, and coyote were taken. Applicants bid for the permits issued and, in the case of muskrats, trapped on a 50 - 50 share basis with the Refuge. The number of permits available each year depended upon the need for controlling excessive populations of these animals.

Faced with the problem of an excessive beaver population which was damaging dikes and water control structures, the Refuge took advantage of the State Conservation Department's first spring beaver trapping season since 1940 and issued fifty trapping permits. This practice was continued for the next several years. In the early 1970's the beaver once again became a nuisance requiring a reduction in their number. Thirty-five were removed the first year, followed by twenty the next.

*Beaver – Seney's First Engineers*　　　　K. SOMMERER

The Refuge muskrat population ranged from being so abundant that it threatened both the stability of the dikes and the successful establishment of marsh and aquatic vegetation to becoming so diminished that in 1962 trapping was discontinued. The peak harvest of 14,000 rats in 1940 and 1941 dwindled to less than 100 in 1962. A reasonable number of muskrats compatible with dike protection and establishment of emergent vegetation was considered desirable, because their feeding on cattail and other wetland emergents created the openings in the marshes so favored by waterfowl. However, the downward trend in muskrat numbers continued in spite of abundant food and potential habitat. This was largely due to the necessity for water level management practices unfavorable to the muskrat. These included seasonal fluctuations in water levels to permit storage of run-off, protection of island goose nesting sites from predators, and exposure of mud flats to induce germination and growth of desirable aquatic plants. From an early policy of seeking to drastically reduce the muskrat population because of its adverse effects on the dikes and marsh plantings, the emphasis has now shifted 180 degrees to encourage it because of its beneficial impact on potential waterfowl habitat.

In 1984 a comprehensive trapping plan was drawn up which provided for recreational trappers to bid on seven trapping units covering 94,850 acres for a three-year period. The objective was to use trapping as a management tool to reduce predation on nesting waterfowl. By the end of the three-year period in 1987, the program was considered sufficiently successful to warrant a second three-year contract beginning in 1988.

Trapping was becoming a much less important activity on the Refuge than it had been in earlier years. The muskrat harvest had diminished significantly to a mere 73 in 1995. Because of the presence of the gray wolf in the Refuge, all coyote trapping was discontinued, and commencing in 1995, only nuisance beaver were trapped. Finally, in 1999 all trapping within the Refuge was terminated.

## Public Trails and Auto Drives Developed

The first signs identifying the area as the Seney National Wildlife Refuge had scarcely been erected before people began coming in streams to see what was happening in the newly-established Refuge. In an attempt to satisfy their interest, an evening motorcade was organized several times a week. A preliminary orientation was presented before the departure of the cars. These motorcades proved quite popular but were criticized for excessive dust from the dirt roads, long lines of cars in the motorcade, and frequently, lack of wildlife seen.

*Seney's Evening Guided Tour*　　　　　USFWS

By the early 1950's one of the most pressing problems confronting the Refuge manager was an exploding number of visitors to the Refuge. From a few hundred it quickly ballooned into thousands, overwhelming Refuge personnel by requiring much of their time and attention. As Henry wrote, "We are rapidly approaching National Park pressure without their facilities." He felt that to avoid undesirable results, i.e. visitor frustrations and disappointments, facilities must be revised, expanded and improved, or else usage by the public terminated. The weekly conducted tours along the seven-mile nature drive through a portion of the Refuge was proving entirely inadequate. Even increasing the schedule to a daily tour was not the answer. Dust was the biggest problem. People in the car line past the sixth vehicle could usually see little wildlife or even scenery because of the cloud of dust raised by preceding cars. Until the tour route could be dust treated (financially prohibitive) Henry felt that "this one condition does much harm to our public relations program." He wrote in his annual report, "when the dust cloud is so thick that they cannot even see the 'Seney scene,' when clothes, autos, faces become covered with grime, we lose far more than we gain." Henry realized that this great amount of interest presented an exceptionally good opportunity to sell the Refuge program to the public, but in order to do so, their trip to the Refuge must be made worthwhile to them. He concluded that the situation must be squarely faced and a thorough reappraisal of Seney's public relations program be made.

Eventually a seven-mile self-guided car route was established open daily during the daylight hours. Over the years this auto tour, which winds past the pools, marshes and upland ridges of Unit 1, continues to be very popular with the public. This Marshland Drive allows the visitor to drive at his own pace aided by informative signs posted along the way pointing to things of interest. As many as 27,000 people enjoy the drive during a typical year.

Another popular trail is the 1-1/2 mile Pine Ridge Nature Trail. This is a walking trail which follows along pine ridges and skirts several pools and marshes. This is very popular, especially with bird watchers; some years as many as 15,000 people hike along this trail.

*School Children at the Start of Seney's Nature Trail* USFWS

In 1992 a new program was started. This was the posting of a summer intern on the Pine Ridge trail or on the Marshland Drive for four hours each day to act as a roving interpreter to answer visitors' questions and to point out special items of interest. This program was well received but was unfortunately terminated in 1995 due to lack of funding for staff.

The Refuge also developed many miles of trails for cross-country skiing and snowshoeing throughout part of the Refuge. This provided a wonderful opportunity for the users of the trails to see the splendor and beauty of the Refuge during the winter months.

But all this was not enough. The number of people visiting the Refuge grew each year. In 1963 the total tally of visitors was 80,000. This increased to 94,015 in

*A Stop Along the Tour*                    USFWS

1971. To answer the needs of the visitors and provide them with a worthwhile and meaningful experience from their visit to the Seney Refuge, the decision was made in 1963 to build a visitor center equipped with wildlife exhibits, books, information and modern equipment for visual presentations - all designed to help the visitors understand and enjoy their visit to the Refuge. The center, a beautiful and modern building overlooking one of the Refuge pools, was completed and dedicated on May 30,1965.

For many years the Refuge had maintained two picnic areas outside the Refuge for the general public. The Wigwam on M-77 was built by the CCC and the WPA in 1937. It consisted of shelter, tables and grills and overlooked the show pools. It was very popular with the traveling public. During 1992 for example, 10,000 people used its facilities. However, in spite of much unfavorable public reaction, it was closed in 1994. Earlier in 1989 the Driggs River picnic area and nature trail on M-28 were closed when the nearby newly-developed state rest area was opened.

*White-tailed Deer*                                                                                    E. LOSEY

## White-tailed Deer

*T*he vast stretch of marsh and woods extending roughly from Seney to Shingleton to the west, collectively known as the "Seney Marsh" has always harbored a substantial number of White-tailed Deer. From very early days these deer were routinely hunted by the first settlers not only for sport but also for food for their families and to supply the many logging camps throughout the area.

With the establishment of the Refuge in 1935 incorporating a large part of this land, deer hunting within the Refuge became subject to certain regulations and restrictions. As always Michigan state game laws were in effect plus certain additional restrictions imposed by the Refuge. For example, some areas within the Refuge were closed to all hunting. This was primarily Unit 1 which comprised those areas containing Refuge buildings and many of the impoundments. Additionally, no baiting was allowed, nor were ATV vehicles permitted. Deer camps could be set up west of the Driggs River only.

The fame of the Refuge for prime deer hunting, particularly during the high deer population years of the 1950's, soon spread. The Refuge became a very popular destination and attracted deer hunters in large numbers not only from all over the state, but also from Ohio and Indiana as well. Germfask was taken over by red-clad hunters. Their pick-ups and cars lined the streets on both sides of the small town. Local restaurants and bars were so crowded that frequently lines of hungry and thirsty men (female hunters were a rarity in those days - although there were a few exceptions) stretched onto the sidewalks outside waiting to gain entry.

This invasion by the large number of deer hunters for the annual fifteen-day state deer season in November presented a perplexing problem for Refuge Manager Henry. In the 1950's the conflict between the Michigan Legislature and the Michigan Conservation Department over management of the deer herd had reached new heights of bitterness and divisiveness. The controversy reached all levels of the public. Modification of the long-standing (and "sacred") principle of "bucks only" to permit the shooting of does evoked violent reaction among all segments of the

*Doe and Fawns*

R. DENOMME

people. Barber shop experts railed against the biologists. Local feelings were bitter and uncompromising. Much of the general public would not accept that the need to keep the number of deer in balance with the available food supply required that does be shot as well as bucks.

In 1953 Henry wrote, "Deer hunting here is still a 'thorn in our side.' It takes a great many man-days of work from essential projects to prepare for and administer this annual invasion and under present conditions we are accomplishing but little beyond tearing up our roads and littering the area with beer cans and other trash. If it were possible to accomplish some deer management at the same time, we would have an entirely different viewpoint. The politicians still reign supreme."

Two years later he repeated his sentiments as follows: "The group advocating sound management is in the minority. The majority just don't want to shoot does. They either refuse to admit there is a problem, or advance some crack-pot scheme as a substitute for sensible

*Sleeping Fawn*

E. LOSEY

management. The Refuge is in a most unfortunate position. There isn't a great deal we can do except drift with the tides."

And again in 1956 he wrote, "Management [deer] is still controlled by the politicians who are interested in votes instead of the welfare of the herd." However, in that same year the door to scientific management was at last opened a crack when the State Legislature finally gave the Con-

*A Doe and Fawns*                    R. DENOMME

servation Department discretionary authority to hold a special any-deer season in certain areas where conditions warranted it.

In his last year as Refuge Manager at Seney (1958), Henry noted in his annual report, "As the period closed, the road crew and maintenance men began the long, costly repair of Refuge roads which has become our annual 'post-deer-hunting-season-hangover'." He concluded by writing, "at this stage of the cycle we have good cause to stop and ponder whether it is worth the cost of the repairs to arrive at the 14th of November with beautiful roads. Then on the 15th the destruction begins which sets us off on a repeat performance the following spring."

Eventually the Michigan Department of Conservation, proponents for sound management based on biological facts freed from political bias, was successful in establishing a balanced pro-

gram for the deer harvest. And after some years, it was gradually accepted by the public.

As the deer population within the Refuge declined from its 1950's high, the number of people hunting in the Refuge has diminished significantly. Many still return to the Refuge for nostalgic reasons - their fathers or grandfathers always hunted there - but realistically, the chances for success in bagging a buck have shifted to the more agricultural areas of the state to the south.

*Typical Deer Hunters' Camp*                    USFWS

# SIX REFUGE MANAGERS
# 1958 - 1973

ollowing the initial construction and development phase of the first quarter century, the next 15 years (1958 - 1973) were characterized by a succession of six Refuge Managers whose administrative term averaged 2.5 years.

## Habitat Improvement and Resource Inventories

outine maintenance was constant and ongoing. Upgrading roads by grading and graveling, stabilizing the dikes and seeding the banks was a continuing process. The original wooden stop-log water control structures were gradually replaced with modern concrete controls. One by one the service buildings were renovated.

A vigorous program of various habitat improvement practices was undertaken. Aquatic waterfowl plants and marsh emergents were planted in designated impoundments. Land was prepared and sown to small grains and cover crops such as oats, rye, buckwheat, corn, brome, alfalfa and clover to create grazing areas for the benefit of geese and upland birds. This was done on a 50-50 partnership basis with participating farmers. By 1967 approximately 500 acres were under cultivation. One large unit of 100 acres, the Diversion Ditch Farm, was cleared and planted to small grains during this period.

An inventory of aquatic plants was regularly made. A system of transect lines was established to form a basis for comparison with subsequent aquatic inventories.

*Diversion Ditch Farm*                                                                                    E. LOSEY

An inventory survey of the entire Refuge was undertaken to determine 1) land development potential, 2) possible new land use, and 3) areas for potential improvement for wildlife. The Refuge was divided into 17 compartments of 5,000 acres each. By 1965, 18,046 acres or 20% of the Refuge had been inventoried. It was finally completed some years later. At that time 25,150 acres amounting to 38% of the Refuge, comprising

*Grass-sedge Marsh*                          E. LOSEY

the western third of the Refuge, were federally designated as a Wilderness Area.

In 1966, for the first time, the Refuge was classified as a fee area under the provisions of the Land and Water Conservation Fund Account. A total of $1,727.00 was collected. This entrance fee was levied for three years until 1969 when it was discontinued. The high cost of implementing the collection system exceeded the anticipated returns. In addition, local criticism was strong. There was also some decline in the amount of visitor use. The fee system was tried once again in 1988, but was discontinued the following year. It still was not financially justifiable.

## Fishing

*A* number of public use activities were carried on at the Refuge at various times. Fishing was one of the most popular offered by the Refuge. This was one which people of all ages could enjoy. In the early days a certain number of pools were open on a rotating basis for fishing during the summer months. A state fishing license was required and state fishing laws were in effect. In addition, no boats were allowed and no lead sinkers or lead-headed jigs could be used. Eventually, a three-mile fishing loop road was established which provided access to the pools regularly open for fishing. During the May 15 to September 30 fishing season the dikes bordering the pools were popular spots for people trying their luck in angling for the pike and perch to be found in the Refuge pools.

*Seney Pike Attract*                          USFWS
*Fishermen (and Women)*

# JOHN FRYE - REFUGE MANAGER
# 1974 - 1981

ohn Frye came to the Refuge in 1974 to begin his seven-year term.

## Walsh Ditch Fire

On July 30, 1976 a bolt of lightning struck and ignited a small one-quarter acre fire in a remote and practically inaccessible part of the Seney Refuge Wilderness Area. Unfortunately this insignificant blaze developed into a great conflagration and a major event of the Refuge's history. Because of difficult access problems, the wet bog location, and the interpretation of wilderness area regulations which stipulated that fire fighting measures not be instituted when no lives or private property were threatened, the decision was made only to monitor the fire because it was thought that it probably would burn itself out in a relatively short time. This did not happen. Quite the contrary. By August 10, more than 1,200 acres had been burned. Obviously a state of emergency existed, so attempts to control the fire were undertaken. Men and heavy fire fighting equipment were brought in. By the time they arrived, August 16, over 17,500 acres had been burned. The Boise Inter-Agency Fire Center was called in. They, along

*Walsh Ditch Fire of 1976*                                                                                    USFWS

with the Forest Fire Division of the Michigan Department of Natural Resources, took over command of the situation.

In spite of all efforts, the fire continued to spread due to a combination of gusty high winds and relatively low humidity. By August 26 the fire still blazed out of control. Over 20,000 acres had been burned. A few days later back fires were started in order to provide zones of burned-over areas which would effectively stop the advancing fire front. These proved successful so that by September 9 the fire was declared to be under control. However, three days later, recurring high gusty winds plus low humidity ignited the smoldering hot spots within the burned perimeter. As a result the blaze exploded north into the Grand Sable Forest and adjoining private forest holdings. Throughout this period a dense pall of smoke covered the area, frequently blanketing the surrounding towns of Seney and Germfask. By September 28 when the fire was finally declared contained, 5,000 men had been involved in the fire fighting and supply and support operations. These people and equipment came from at least 29 states. A total of 75,000 acres were burned of which 57,000 were within the Seney Refuge, 16,250 acres in State forest lands, and 1,750 in private lands. The total cost to control the fire was eight million dollars.

The Seney fire of 1976 will long be remembered. The big question was, what were its effects on the Refuge wildlife and its habitat? The smoking embers had hardly cooled before steps were taken to determine the fire's impact. A special team of biologists was called in to make a preliminary survey and appraisal of its immediate significance. A three-year long range research program was set up to evaluate all aspects of the fire as it impacted the wildlife population, habitat, soil and water conditions on the burned and unburned areas.

In brief, the results of the study showed that overall the fire was beneficial to wildlife. It created greater diversity of wildlife habitat by setting back natural succession, maintaining open areas, creating edge, elimination of understory and creation of snags and downed logs. No species was destroyed completely or eliminated because no habitat was totally destroyed. Another important benefit from the fire was the removal of the large amount of accumulated debris on the ground plus the standing dead vegetation which, when left unburned, provides a potential explosive fire hazard. In fact, total

*Advancing Fireline*　　　　　　　　　　USFWS

*Airplane Dropping Flame Retardant on the Walsh Ditch Fire* USFWS

exclusion of fire carries the risk of build-up of accumulation of fuel from materials to such an extent that a widespread high intensive fire results which can cause loss of floral and faunal diversity.

The Walsh Ditch Fire, as the 1976 blaze was called, was the major event of the year. Its impact was tremendous measured in terms of cost in money, man-hours, and disruption of normal Refuge operations. However, the overall lasting effect was actually beneficial. For the fire, by setting back the natural succession of tree and plant growth, created a highly desirable greater diversity of wildlife habitat favored by many species of wildlife.

Seven years after the Walsh Ditch fire of 1976, fire once again struck the Seney Refuge. The summer of 1983 was the driest and warmest ever experienced in the eastern Upper Peninsula in over 24 years. On August 14 a major wildfire occurred in a remote area a mile southwest of Marsh Creek pool. Prompt action enabled the fire to be contained within three days, but it was not until October 5 that it was declared totally extinguished. Fire suppression costs totaled between $400,000 and $450,000. It also caused major disruption of many normal Refuge activities. Because of the fire's remote location and the extreme drought conditions, it had all the potential of becoming as large and costly as the 1976 Seney Walsh Ditch fire.

Employing the necessary precautions and safeguards, the use of fire as a means of creating certain desired types of habitat is very beneficial. For example, using controlled burning to remove brush and sapling growth produces conditions and openings favorable for upland game birds, such as Sharp-tailed Grouse, Woodcock, Canada Geese and Sandhill Cranes as well as a number of species of sparrows. Fire has proved to be a most valuable management tool.

## Sharp-tailed Grouse

From the very early days of the Refuge's establishment, attention was paid to the needs of upland game birds, especially Sharp-tailed Grouse. These birds were found chiefly in open grassland-poplar country in the north part of the Refuge adjacent to open land owned by the Michigan Department of Natural Resources just south of M-28. In the 1950's and 1960's the sharptail population reached an all-time high. Although hunting for these birds was never allowed within the Refuge, it was permitted on state lands. Hunters from far and wide quickly took advantage of this opportunity for some fabulous sport. On the opening day of bird season, hunters' cars were parked on each side of M-28 for several miles west of

Seney. Promptly at 7:00 a.m. (opening time) the hunters and their dogs began moving slowly through the state area. As they proceeded, the sharptails they flushed flew in flocks of six to twelve south toward the sanctuary of the Refuge. One hunter (the author) and her husband stationed themselves just north of the Refuge line the night before opening day and so were well positioned for some excellent pass shooting as the birds flew overhead toward the Refuge.

Unfortunately, the population of Sharp-tailed Grouse did not remain at a high level. In spite of many management practices designed to maintain and improve their habitat, their numbers slowly diminished. In an effort to reverse this trend, desirable openings in Sharp-tailed Grouse habitat were maintained and new ones created by a combination of small controlled

*Sharp-tailed Grouse*

R. BAETSEN

burns, use of large mowers, brushing and timber removal. In addition, under a system of crop sharing 228 acres of upland were cultivated and planted with assorted grains and grasses such as crested wheat grass, brome, red-top and buckwheat. Haying was also used as a management tool on approximately 415 acres to provide the legume-grass areas that were favored not only by grouse but also by Canada Geese, Sandhill Cranes, deer and bear. Land was prepared and sown to small grains and cover crops to create grazing areas for the benefit of geese and upland birds.

*Sharp-tailed Grouse Dancing Ground*

E. LOSEY

This was done on a 50-50 partnership basis with participating farmers. By 1967, approximately 500 acres were under cultivation.

A census of Sharp-tailed Grouse dancing grounds (leks) was taken on a regular basis. The results showed that in spite of all management efforts, both the number of dancing grounds as well as the total grouse population was on a downward trend. The irreversible encroachment of brush into grouse range continued relentlessly eliminating much prime grouse habitat.

Reflecting this decline in 1973 the Michigan Department of Conservation closed the entire county of Schoolcraft to Sharp-tailed Grouse hunting. The Refuge, however, refused to give up its efforts to create habitat that would favor and promote an increase in the Sharp-tailed Grouse population. Using a combination of timber-cutting and prescribed burning to create large scale openings favorable especially for sharptails as well as deer, Sandhill Cranes, Canada Geese, and various non-game birds, a large 1800-acre opening in the Diversion Farm south of the diversion ditch in the northcentral section of the Refuge was created. The trees were cut and burned leaving a combination of slash, an open meadow and one area of uncut woodland.

Subsequent observations (in the 1990's) have shown that wildlife, especially Sharp-tailed Grouse, have responded favorably to this environment. For example, in 1998, twenty-nine displaying sharptails were counted on the dancing ground. In fact, this combination of burning and cutting holds much promise for the future of the Sharp-tailed Grouse and will be utilized wherever conditions warrant it.

*Prairie Chicken*                R. BAETSEN

Although a small number of sharptails are still present in the Refuge, the few Prairie Chickens that once were found within the Refuge as well as in a small area north of M-28 known as the Bullock Farm, have completely disappeared. The last Prairie Chicken was seen on C-3 dike in 1951. The noise of their booming is now just a memory for those lucky enough to have heard it.

One of the rewards for the author when censusing the Sharp-tailed Grouse on the Refuge in 1951 is the memory of a night spent in a small pup tent within a few yards of a sharptail dancing ground. At daybreak the male birds began arriving into the area. One even perched for some time on top of my tent. One by one the birds assembled until about eight or ten were gathered on their dancing ground - a small spot on a low knoll pounded bare by many years of use by the birds. The sharptails, emitting their cackling call, began rapidly stamping their feet, running about in all directions, inflating the brilliant purple-colored sacs on each side of their

*Dancing Sharp-tailed Grouse*                                                                                    R. BAETSEN

neck, all the while rattling their erect tail feathers as they danced about with their wings lowered and held stiffly at their sides. In the quiet stillness of the early morning their calls were audible for several miles. It is everyone's hope that this colorful spectacle of early spring will always be a part of our natural heritage.

# STATE AND FEDERAL PROGRAMS

Commencing in 1975 and extending throughout the 90's several state and federal programs became available to the Refuge. The first program in which the Refuge participated was that of the Government funded Youth Conservation Corps (YCC). This was a program designed to give training and work experience to young people from the local area. They were chosen in a random drawing at a public meeting. For a period of six to eight weeks they performed a wide variety of tasks under the supervision of Refuge personnel. A partial list of the work they did included fence repairs, fence brushing, clearing goose nesting islands, assisting in farming operations, helping at the visitor center, building foot bridges and bridge railings, painting buildings, planting trees, mulching ditch dikes, live trapping and banding geese, and posting the Refuge boundary. Their work over the four years the program continued was invaluable and contributed a great deal to the successful operation of the Refuge. To this day many local residents speak fondly of the summer they spent at the Refuge as a YCC participant.

In addition to the YCC program, there were the Michigan Youth Corps and the Student Conservation Association all of which offered opportunities for learning and training at the Refuge for the local youth. Also there was the Young Adult Conservation Corps, a federally funded program. They built the Riverside Road buildings that served as their headquarters.

For adults there were a variety of programs such as the Green Thumb Program, the Retired Senior Volunteer Program, and the Seney National Wildlife Refuge Volunteers. The many hours they donated and the many tasks they performed contributed substantially to various Refuge projects and activities, particularly in the public use program.

# DONALD FRICKIE - REFUGE MANAGER
# 1981 - 1988

*J*n 1981 Donald Frickie came to the Refuge as its tenth manager. He initiated a wide range of biological programs. An aquatic inventory of all twenty-one impoundments was taken on a regular basis. Planting of aquatics was done where needed. A systematic drawdown of pools was carried out on a rotating basis. This not only aerated the pools but also promoted a lush growth of small aquatics, such as needle rush, on the exposed pool bottoms. They were a source of food heavily used by Canada Geese, waterfowl, Sandhill Cranes, shorebirds and other wildlife.

The 22,884 acres of forest habitat were inventoried according to type and a plan developed to reestablish forest openings in certain areas that would enhance wildlife habitat.

A major effort was undertaken to rehabilitate waterfowl nesting islands by extensive clearing and brushing. Also twenty-seven miles of pool dikes were mowed and burned to provide goose grazing areas.

After fifty years of use the Refuge headquarters building underwent a major remodeling and renovation. By enclosing the three garage vehicle bays, the office space was more than doubled. The exterior of the entire building was sheathed with cedar paneling and enhanced with attractive landscape plantings. The work was completed in 1988.

*Administration Building*

E. LOSEY

## Cooperative Agreements

rickie's eight-year tenure was marked by a series of cooperative agreements between the Refuge and a number of agencies such as the Michigan Department of Natural Resources (DNR), the Ohio Cooperative Wildlife Research Unit, the State of Michigan, and the local Community Action Agency.

The agreement with the DNR covered many areas in which participation and assistance on the part of both agencies would benefit wildlife. Examples were habitat improvement measures using mowing and burning to create and maintain openings favored by upland birds such as Sharp-tailed Grouse, Woodcock and Sandhill Cranes; mutual coordination of efforts in fire fighting; preliminary planning on the Fisher reintroduction program; initiating and evaluating methods for censusing Black Bears; and a program for color marking and banding loons.

# WILDLIFE RESEARCH

rom the very beginning of the Refuge's establishment, a variety of management practices and research projects designed to better understand the needs of the diverse wildlife found within its borders were initiated by the Refuge Managers. Both Refuge and outside independent biologists participated in these studies. In most cases the results of their research were published in appropriate scientific journals.

*Hooded Merganser*                    R. BAETSEN

Boxes put up in trees to encourage nesting by Wood Ducks proved to be occupied largely by Hooded Mergansers and squirrels. To restore and encourage the Common Tern population

*Ring-necked Ducks*          R. DENOMME

various methods and devices were employed such as wooden tern decoys, taped colonial nesting calls, herbicides to reduce vegetation, addition of gravel to enhance nesting sites and even constructing a predator deterring fence around a potential nesting island. But in spite of all these efforts, no appreciable increase in Common Tern nesting was achieved, so the program was gradually phased out. Detailed research by John Sarvis on the Ring-necked Duck examining its life history and habitat requirements was successfully completed.

Beaver Pond – Prime Waterfowl Habitat          E. LOSEY

Beaver                         R. DENOMME

The importance of beaver in waterfowl management and duck brood behavior under natural conditions were subjects of research. From the day of their first arrival at the Refuge, the Canada Goose flock was studied including all phases of its life history, its habitat requirements and causes of mortality. The habits of the river otter were examined. An intensive study into all phases of Black Duck management was initiated. It covered habitat requirements for nesting and brood rearing, techniques for censusing, breeding pairs and broods, and management strategies for improving their habitat.

Mallard Duck with Young          R. BAETSEN

The Refuge developed a working relationship with the Ohio State Cooperative Wildlife Research Unit. Under the leadership of Dr. Ted Bookhout several major studies were conducted. The long-term Yellow Rail project commenced in 1979, is ongoing with a prescribed burn to enhance the rails' habitat scheduled for 2002.

American Widgeon          J. SARVIS

Two-day old Black Duckling          E. LOSEY

*Sandhill Crane on Nest*

## Whooping Crane Project

*I*n 1984 a major long range program was initiated. This was the Whooping Crane project. Its goal was to establish a secondary migratory Whooping Crane flock in the eastern United States distinct from the western one (Wood Buffalo Park, Northwest Territories - Aransas Refuge, Texas). If successful, this flock would be insurance against the only self-sustaining migratory Whooping Crane population presently in existence being wiped out by some catastrophe. The plan involved using the Refuge's Sandhill Crane population in a cross-fostering plan with Whooping Cranes whereby Whooping Crane eggs would be placed in Sandhill Crane nests and the chicks reared by the Sandhill Cranes. They would then be trained to follow the ultra-light aircraft from their rearing area in the north to a selected wintering area in Florida. Sandhill Cranes were chosen to test the feasibility of this plan.

First, however, it was necessary to study all aspects of the Seney population of Sandhill Cranes. The following had to be determined: size of breeding population, reproductive success of nesting pairs, movements of marked cranes, identification of staging areas, migration routes and wintering sites.

The Sandhill Crane-Whooping Crane project first begun in 1984 in cooperation with Dr. Ted Bookhout of the Ohio Cooperative Fish and Wildlife Research Unit with the assistance of Janet L. McMillen. Its immediate objective was to develop a re-introduction technique for a migratory population of Whooping Cranes. As a first step Sandhill Cranes were to be used as a surrogate species. Using a technique devised by Dr. Richard Urbanek, the cranes were raised totally free from visible human contact. This was achieved by isolation rearing and the use of puppet crane heads and complete camouflage for human handlers. When grown, the captive-reared chicks were to be released into a local flock of wild Sandhill Cranes, hopefully to become assimilated and as an integral part of the flock, migrate south in the fall and return to the Refuge in the spring.

From 1988 through 1990, thirty-eight color-marked and radio-tagged captive-reared Sandhill Cranes were released into the wild. In 1990, thirty-two captive-reared cranes returned to the Refuge proving that isolation-reared cranes released into a flock of their own species could survive and return to their natal area. To date, this was the only successful experimental release of a large number of Sandhill Cranes in a migratory situation that has ever been performed. These cranes demonstrated high survival, appropriate migration and wintering behavior, high return rate and successful reproduction.

R. DENOMME

Further testing and development of the reliability of this isolation-puppet rearing technique was needed. Because of the unavailability of Whooping Crane eggs, in 1991 18 Red-Crowned Cranes were chosen as an experimental surrogate to be raised by the same methods. Unfortunately this experiment had to be aborted when one of the chicks tested weakly positive for presence of a virus that later was not confirmed, thus preventing their release into the wild.

*Puppet Feeding of Captive Isolation-Reared Chick*

J. REUTHER

Sandhill Cranes

R. DENOMME

In 1994 the U.S. Whooping Crane Recovery Team, while commenting favorably on the progress made in developing techniques currently being carried on at the Seney National Wildlife Refuge, declined to approve the continuation of the work at Seney. Instead they mandated that any new proposed research be performed by different personnel in a different location.

A year later the Sandhill Crane-Whooping Crane Program was enlarged to combine isolation rearing and the use of ultra-light aircraft into a reintroduction method that could ultimately be used to reestablish Whooping Cranes in parts of their currently unoccupied former range.

Dr. Urbanek Feeding Cranes Using Puppet Crane Head

J. REUTHER

In 1996 the Fish and Wildlife Service gave Seney Refuge lead responsibility for coordinating Whooping Crane recovery activities in Region 3. At the same time Biologist Dr. Richard Urbanek was designated Regional Whooping Crane contact.

Once again Sandhill Cranes were to be used to test the feasibility of the program. Necedah Wildlife Refuge in northcentral Wisconsin was named as the area for the isolation-puppet raising of the chicks and the subsequent training to follow the ultra-light planes on migratory flights to Chassahowitzka Refuge on the northwest coast of Florida which had been chosen as wintering area. In 2000 this program was able to demonstrate successfully that Sandhill Cranes could be trained to follow ultra-light aircraft the complete length of this migration route.

Finally, in the summer of 2001 forty-seven 64-day-old Whooping Crane chicks hatched from eggs at the Patuxent National Wildlife Refuge arrived at Necedah. This represented the final step in the 17-year long Sandhill Crane-Whooping Crane Recovery Program. The chicks were isolation-reared and trained to follow ultra-light planes. On October 17, 2001 at 7:15 a.m. a group of eight young Whooping Cranes left the Necedah National Wildlife Refuge in Wisconsin following, as they had been trained to do, two ultra-light aircraft. They were on the first leg of their long journey designed to teach them a route to wintering grounds at the Chassahowitzka

National Wildlife Refuge in northwestern Florida. On December 4 the birds successfully reached their destination after flying a distance of 1,218 miles.

During their winter sojourn two of the birds were killed by bobcats. On April 9, 2002 the five surviving Whooping Cranes left the Florida Refuge to begin their migration north. After ten anxious-filled days, the people at Necedah Refuge on April 19 were overjoyed to see their five Whooping Cranes circle high overhead before gracefully gliding down for a safe return to their natal home. Because of this successful outcome, a second similar program of rearing the birds for ultra-light guided flights to Chassahowitzka National Wildlife Refuge in the fall of 2002 will again be undertaken.

*Sandhill Crane at Nest with Chick and Egg*     R. DENOMME

## Trumpeter Swans

*O*n May 16, 1991 another event of great importance took place at the Seney Refuge. Ten two-year old Trumpeter Swans were released in several of the Refuge impoundments. This was the first step in a program sponsored by the Michigan Department of Natural Resources Natural History Program in cooperation with the Fish and Wildlife Service in an effort to reintroduce the Trumpeter Swan as a breeding bird to the State of Michigan.

In 1989, twenty Trumpeter Swan eggs had been collected from wild swans nesting in Alaska. These eggs were hatched and the cygnets raised at Michigan State University's Kellogg Bird Sanctuary near Battle Creek, Michigan. Now after two years in captivity, ten of these

R. DENOMME

swans were to begin their new life in the Refuge. It was hoped that they would adapt to their new environment so that they would "imprint" on their new surroundings and, when forced to leave the area during freeze-up, would return the following year to establish territories within the Refuge.

Seney Refuge had been chosen as a swan release site for two reasons: first it was largely free of power lines potentially dangerous to flying birds; second it was a lead-free environment. Because no waterfowl hunting had ever been allowed in the Refuge since 1947, its pools were free of the lead shot so lethal to waterfowl when they accidentally ingest it.

The success of the Trumpeter Swan program was soon evident. In 1992, the first year after release, two cygnets were fledged. This represented the first documented breeding of Trumpeter Swans in the Upper Peninsula since the species was extirpated in the late 1880's. Also that year, twenty-three additional two-year olds were released in the Refuge. The following year, because

*Trumpeter Swan on Nest*

K. SOMMERER

of a surplus of females, three additional males were added to balance the sex ratio of the Refuge flock. Four cygnets were successfully hatched and fledged that year. From then on, the number of adults steadily increased as did the number of cygnets produced. Seven years later (1998) there were 76 of these majestic white birds at home on the Seney pools. By 2002 the number of adult swans had increased to 166. For that same year, 68 cygnets were produced of which 37 survived to flight stage.

*Trumpeter Swan Family*

K. SOMMERER

*Common Loon*

J. GAVIN

## Common Loon

*T*he Common Loon has become a threatened species within Michigan, its numbers currently estimated at less than 700 breeding pairs. The largest and healthiest nesting population of loons in the eastern part of the Upper Peninsula is found in the Seney Refuge.

By the late 1990's the Seney Refuge's population of loons had reached full carrying capacity. Nearly every pool of sufficient size and habitat was occupied by a pair of Common Loons. This was in marked contrast to the surrounding eastern Upper Peninsula where occupancy of lakes was no higher than 20%. In 2001 not only was the nesting of thirteen pairs a Refuge record, but so also was the hatching of sixteen chicks.

In 1989 Seney was chosen by David Evers of the Whitefish Point Bird Observatory to be the site for a long-term continuing study into various aspects of loon biology. The objective was wide ranged: to collect data on breeding behavior, population dynamics, survivorship, seasonal movement, territory establishment, pair fidelity, return rate, and impact of environmental contaminants, such as mercury levels.

Evers, along with Biologists Joe Kaplan and Damon McCormick, was able to devise the first successful time-efficient, night lighting, low-risk capture technique for adult loons in nesting territory. After several seasons of work, the captured birds became the first color-marked breeding population of Common Loons in North America. This color-marked population at Seney was one of only eight areas currently being studied in the Great Lakes region.

This program of color banding has made it possible to acquire a great deal of information about loon behavior as well as some amazing life histories of individual birds. The myth that loons mate for life has been dispelled. It has also been established that they are a long-lived

*Common Loon with Chicks*  R. BAETSEN

species. One female returned to her same territory for thirteen consecutive years, during which time she had paired with at least four different males.

In 2002, for the first time a third generation loon was identified. His lineage was traced from his 15-year old father, who as of 2002, is still an active breeder and who is the oldest loon of known age in North America, and from his grandfather who was the first adult loon ever color-banded on the Refuge.

In 1996 Dr. Charles Walcott of Cornell University began his research into the yodel calls of male loons. Yodel calls are given only by male loons, and significantly each male loon has its own characteristic yodel that is different in both frequency and timing from all other males in the population. These yodel calls appear to be associated with maintenance of territory.

Dr. Walcott's research appeared to suggest that a male loon changes its yodel if it changes its territory. Therefore, identification of a male loon by its characteristic yodel loses its validity when the loon moves into a new territory. Research on this interesting aspect of loon behavior is continuing.

## Yellow Rail

The rare Yellow Rail, one of the most sought after birds to be found at Seney remains the focus of several studies. Dr. Ted Bookhout of Ohio State Cooperative Fish and Wildlife Unit continued his analysis, which he had begun in 1979, of its population status and habitat use. Rails were captured and banded, type of habitat used by breeding males was determined, and the possibility of using counts of males' calls as an accurate meas-

*Burned Area for Yellow Rail Study*  T. & J. REUTHER

*Banded Yellow Rail*                                                    J. HOLLINGSWORTH

ure of breeding density was investigated. In 1995 the distinctive tck-tck call of 84 male Yellow Rails was heard. This was the highest number ever heard during any previous breeding season at Seney. The following year only five were heard; in 1997 the number dropped to one, but increased to eight in 1998. This high degree of fluctuation in number was not considered unusual, since it has been found that Yellow Rails are a species which does not exhibit site fidelity. Also, the high degree of variability in weather conditions during April and May may influence the extent to which the Refuge is used by the rails.

Peggy Burkman's research on the Yellow Rail showed that open sedge marshes characterized by mat-forming sedge were their preferred habitat. Next the effect of prescribed burning to maintain these marshes was evaluated. A comparison of population densities on burned and unburned areas indicated that calling males showed a preference for the burned areas. The use of prescribed fire apparently can be a valuable tool in maintaining this desirable Yellow Rail habitat.

## Kirtland's Warbler

*I*n 1990 the management of Fish and Wildlife Service-owned tracts in lower Michigan was transferred to the Seney Refuge. This involved land management on 119 separate tracts totaling 6,684 acres in an eight-county area around Grayling in lower Michigan. The Kirtland's Warbler, one of the world's rarest birds, is found in young jack pine stands growing in this area.

The warbler's requirements for nesting are very specific. They nest only in jack pine forests that are about 80 acres or larger with a scattering of numerous small grassy openings. The trees must be between five to sixteen feet tall and so spaced as to let sunlight reach the ground thus creating the necessary open spots.

*Singing Male Kirtland's Warbler*                                                R. BAETSEN

Management efforts are directed to maintaining and increasing the amount of this type of habitat. Because of the scattered distribution of the small tracts and the presence of many homes throughout the same area, plus the highly explosive nature of jack pine, the prescribed burning to create fire regenerated jack pine is not generally practical. Therefore, clear cutting of jack pine, followed by direct seeding or planting are the primary options available to establish the desired stands of young jack pine. Since these Kirtland's Warbler tracts are too small to be managed individually, they are regenerated in cooperation and in a coordinated fashion with the Michigan Department of Natural Resources' timber harvesting plans for adjacent lands. Seney Refuge personnel are responsible for the cutting and regeneration of these small tracts. They also conduct a yearly census of the birds. Results of the 1998 census were an encouraging record high of 804 singing males, which was a 10.4% increase over 1997. The number of singing males for 2001 rose to a new recorded high of 1,077.

A serious problem confronting the successful management of the Kirtland's Warbler is the large Brown-headed Cowbird population. These birds commonly lay their eggs in the Kirtland's Warbler nests. Because of their much larger size, the cowbird young crowd out and starve the weaker and smaller Kirtland's Warbler nestlings. This parasitism results in substantial loss of the Kirtland's Warbler nestlings. An ongoing effort is being made to remove as many cowbirds as possible by intensive trapping. This practice has yielded encouraging results. In fact, since 1972 when the program of trapping cowbirds was begun, 108,452 cowbirds have been trapped and killed. The average annual harvest is 4,017. The survival of the Kirtland's Warbler will depend on continued cowbird control as exercised by Fish and Wildlife personnel as well as intensive (and extensive) habitat management.

## Satellite Refuges

*Bald Eagle*                    K. SOMMERER

*J*n the 1980's the Seney Refuge was given the responsibility of administering and managing several small wildlife Refuges. They are groups of islands located in the Great Lakes which are all part of the National Wildlife Refuge System. These islands are Harbor Island National Wildlife Refuge, a 695-acre island located one mile north of Drummond Island in Lake Huron; Michigan Island National Wildlife Refuge, a group of four islands totaling 245 acres located in the northern portion of Lake Michigan; and Huron Island National Wildlife Refuge consisting of eight islands totaling 147 acres situated eighteen miles east of the Keweenaw Peninsula on the south side of Lake Superior.

These Great Lakes islands contain a wide diversity of habitats and wildlife that are unique and fragile. Each is rugged and rocky. Their vegetation is stunted in most areas due to the shallow soils and windy nature of the islands. Because of their remoteness and difficulty of access, they each share freedom from most human disturbance. In the summer the islands are alive with the calls of gulls, terns, herons, cormorants and breeding songbirds. Bald Eagles, Great Grey Owls and Peregrine Falcons have also been observed. The Refuge staff makes regular visits to monitor the wildlife and check the overall condition of the islands.

# MICHAEL G. TANSY - REFUGE MANAGER 1989 - 2001

*M*ichael G. Tansy began his twelve-year term as Manager of the Seney National Wildlife Refuge in 1989. During his administration a number of important biological studies and major habitat modifications were either initiated or advanced. Examples were the Trumpeter Swan reintroduction, continuous research on Common Loon, Sandhill Crane, Yellow Rail and Kirtland's Warbler as well as innovative practices in landscape management. Cooperative agreements with numerous public agencies were continued.

## Neo-tropical Migratory Bird Research Programs

*C*ommencing in 1990 Seney Refuge became an active participant in various programs designed to study the causes of the serious decline in numbers of neo-tropical migratory birds. "Partners in Flight" was a coordinated international cooperative effort for neo-tropical bird conservation. Its objectives were to determine the status and specific causes of neo-tropical migratory bird decline, to maintain stable populations, and to reverse declining population trends through habitat restoration and enhancement. To carry out these objectives, three new long term surveys were begun at Seney.

LeConte's Sparrow                    R. BURNARD

The first was the Breeding Bird Survey. This was a non-random twenty-five-mile road route of fifty stops established to cover most Refuge habitats, both upland and wetland. This route is to be run each year and will yield long-term data on bird population trends.

The second survey was the Hiawatha Breeding Bird Survey. It was a cooperative effort to gather information on bird populations of the Central Upper Peninsula. Groups of interested birders throughout the state participated in this survey. On the Seney Refuge two transects, each containing twelve points at one-mile intervals, were established and run on two consecutive days. These transects were oriented along the Pine Creek and Driggs River roads.

MAPS (Monitoring Avian Productivity and Survivorship) was the third survey in which the Seney Refuge participated. MAPS was a cooperative effort among public agencies, private organizations and the bird banders of North America to provide long-term data on population and demographic parameters of selected target land bird species in each of seven major regions of the continent. The program uses standardized constant-effort mist netting and banding and standardized point counts during the breeding season at a continent-wide network of stations. A permanent plot was established in alder-sedge habitat on the north side of J-1 pool. This was a major habitat in the Refuge area not otherwise represented in the regional MAPS program.

Great Blue Heron                    K. SOMMERER

Osprey                    T. REUTHER

# Rehabilitation of Driggs River

The first of two projects carried out by Tansy was a much needed restoration of the Driggs River which was carried out in 1994. This river runs about fifteen miles through the center of the Refuge before joining the Manistique River and eventually emptying into Lake Michigan. About a century ago pine logs were floated down the river to mill sites on Lake Michigan. In driving the logs down the river,

*Erosion Bank Stabilization*                                        USFWS

all of the woody debris in the river was removed. This woody debris had provided a certain amount of stream bank stability as well as shelter for insects and fish. Over the years deposition of sand into the river from the badly eroded and scoured banks has resulted. Fifty-two sites were identified as needing protection. As part of the rehabilitation process, cuttings of willow, alder, red-osier dogwood, and sweet gale were planted along these eroded sites in May. During August and September these severely eroded bank sites encompassing over one linear mile of river bank were rehabilitated with tree revetments. These revetments were constructed by placing entire red and jack pine trees into the river bed at the base of the eroded bank. Sites with undercut banks were then fertilized and replanted with red pine. Although the planting of cuttings exhibited good viability the first year, their survival rate after that was quite low. Beavers destroyed some of the cuttings. Bank instability either washed out or buried most of the remaining cuttings. However, the tree revetment project was very successful in reducing erosion at the fifty-two eroded outside river curves as well as improving fish habitats.

*Rehabilitation of Eroded River Bank*                    M. TANSY

# Restoration of Marsh Creek Watershed

*I*n 2001 the Refuge awarded a construction contract which will result over the next several years in the restoration of thousands of acres of drained wetlands to their original state. In 1915 the Walsh Ditch cut through these wetlands in an attempt to develop the area for agriculture. The project was unsuccessful because of the peat-sand soils and the short growing season. Twenty years later, the Seney National Wildlife Refuge was established on land which had been acquired by the Fish and Wildlife Service.

The Walsh Ditch is sixteen miles long and flows through the heart of the roadless wetland portion of the Refuge's western half. The effects of the ditch on its surroundings are both many and important. A major result has been the lowering of ground water levels next to the ditch. This allows the peat soils to decay and burn. Lower ground water levels have also caused changes in vegetation permitting woody species of trees and shrubs to take over naturally wet open sedge grasslands and marshes. In addition, surface flows of vast quantities of snow melt water that, before the ditch was dug, gradually flowed to the southeast spreading over the area, have been stopped and are now funneled quickly down the ditch. During spring run-off the ditch banks erode and discharge a large volume of sand sediments into the Manistique River.

The restoration plan involves returning the flow of water to both historic channels of Marsh and Walsh Creeks, whose stream flows had been cut off with the digging of the Walsh Ditch. Peak spring water flows in the Driggs River will double in volume as this project restores the river to its historic condition. Construction of three new water control structures and installation of several ditch plugs will complete the stream restoration.

*Mike Tansy at Marsh Creek Restoration Area*    E. LOSEY

Although it will take several years to see the results of this restoration of water to Marsh and Walsh Creeks and the Driggs River, it is confidently expected that the project will help restore the wilderness area's primeval character. Once water flow is returned, the natural hydrology of the area should return, and peat soil should start a rebuilding process. Restoration will improve habitat for beaver and wildlife, especially waterfowl, which will benefit from beaver ponds. Less sand will flow into the Manistique River. Habitat will be improved for species requiring large open wet grasslands.

This project of restoring "the wet to wetlands" is one of major importance and goes a long way toward realizing the Seney Refuge's potential for providing the most favorable conditions for a large variety of wildlife.

*Water Diversion Unit Under Construction*                    E. LOSEY

## Geographic Information System

An important long-term on-going project is being carried on by Refuge staff to produce an accurate Geographic Information System (GIS) cover map of the Refuge. This has high priority since these maps have become a base required by a wide variety of wildlife and environmental habitat studies. In 1997 an interesting project was initiated, designed to develop a predictive model that associated bird species with habitat cover type. This study utilized breeding bird data gained from point counts and habitat data from the Refuge GIS cover map.

The model developed will allow management to make more informed decisions concerning changes in bird populations that might result from management actions. This use of the Refuge GIS cover map as a management tool to predict bird community data will be evaluated.

## Refuge Policy and Management Practices

In 1989 conforming to the newly revised guidelines of the Fish and Wildlife Service, a major shift in Refuge policy was introduced. Waterfowl were no longer to be the Refuge's primary concern. Instead, a new approach based on biodiversity was adopted. This was a recognition that wildlife is one complete organism composed of many diverse and interdependent forms. It therefore required an ecosystem approach both to land management and to the stewardship of its wildlife, fish and plants which recognized this mutual interlocking relationship.

As always, the water levels in the Refuge pools are monitored closely. They are manipulated by raising, lowering or even draining the pools to create habitat diversity and increase wetland productivity by encouraging the growth of the wetland emergent vegetation so favored by waterfowl, geese and cranes. In addition, the pools are mapped and surveys taken of the aquatic plants. This is necessary to show the amount and variety of aquatic food plants present in the pools.

Commencing in 1989 and extending over several years, an effort was made to encourage nesting by Black Terns. To accomplish this, a number of small platforms constructed of wood and wire filled with mud and vegetation and designed to simulate the natural floating mats favored by birds were placed in several of the Refuge pools. After seven years, this practice was discontinued as being unproductive. There was no shortage of natural floating mat nests in the

*Black Tern Sitting on a Nest*                R. BAETSEN

pools, and although large numbers of these were regularly destroyed by high waters, the Black Terns did not appear to use the artificial platforms as substitutes for the natural sites.

In addition to various surveys of song bird populations, a routine censusing of American Woodcock, Ruffed Grouse and waterfowl is performed on a regular basis. Sharp-tailed Grouse are studied to evaluate the success of a number of management practices.

A long-range program for cutting several diversified types of habitat utilizing the removal of trees has begun. In the first 200-acre tract, the entire area has been clear cut to set the succession back to its very early stage of grass and brush, thereby resulting in conditions favorable for Sharp-tailed Grouse and other grassland species such as several species of sparrows and Bobolinks. In the second 140-acre parcel, all trees have been removed except oak to create savanna-like conditions, and in the third 180-acre area only the red pine has been left standing. As these areas mature, the habitats created will be able to fill a very specific niche in wildlife habitat.

In 1998 a major step was taken with the purchase of a modern herbarium to house the Refuge collection of plants accumulated over the years. It now contains over 500 specimens with especial representation of aquatic vegetation. Under the capable supervision of Dr. Richard McNeill the collection is now being rehabilitated, checked for accuracy of identification, and properly catalogued. A concerted drive is presently under way to eradicate the invasive exotic plants that are growing in increasing abundance throughout the Refuge. Species such as glossy buckthorn and spotted knapweed are being especially targeted.

*American Woodcock*                R. BAETSEN

# SENEY NATURAL HISTORY ASSOCIATION

*J*n 1987 the Lake States Cooperative Association which had been operating the bookstore in the visitor center since 1979 posted a record sales of $24,603. The following year it turned over its inventory and operation to the newly-formed Seney Natural History Association.

The Seney Natural History Association was organized in 1987. Its start was made possible by a $10,000 three-year interest-free loan from the National Fish and Wildlife Foundation and by the donation from the Lakeside Interpretive Association of their 1987 end-of-the-year stock of books and tapes.

The broad purpose of the Seney Natural History Association as stated in its by-laws is, "to promote a better understanding and appreciation of the natural history and natural environment of the Upper Peninsula of Michigan, and in particular, the Seney National Wildlife Refuge." Specifically, its primary objective is to support Refuge projects. Funding is made possible through donations and the sale of suitable interpretive and educational materials such as books, tapes, and souvenirs. In addition, the Association also undertakes to acquire the books, films, recordings and other materials needed for interpretive and environmental programs and to assist the Refuge in carrying out such programs.

The Association's gross sales, which over an eleven-year period averaged $68,000 per year, were realized from their bookstore. These funds were expended in a variety of projects

*Visitors Using Observation Deck with Interpretive Panels*　　　　　　　　　E. LOSEY

designed to assist the Refuge. Chief among these was the Association sponsorship of the intern program. Commencing in 1992 the Seney Natural History Association funded a number of twelve-week internships offering housing and $50 per week for each qualified applicant that was accepted. Over the years the number of interns increased from four to eight and the weekly stipend was gradu-

*Line Up for Fish Dinner* USFWS

ally increased to $150 per week. These internships were usually equally divided between public use interns and wildlife biology interns. Their contributions were significant and quite invaluable in carrying out activities and programs in the visitor center and in assisting the Refuge biologist with a variety of his responsibilities such as surveys and wildlife research. Other projects underwritten by the Association were the construction of a blind for wildlife photographers, purchase of observation scopes and binoculars for use by the visitors, funding materials needed for month-

ly special events, and underwriting the cost of the food for various functions such as the annual Children's Fishing Day and Volunteers' Awards Banquet. The Association also funds the cost of some Refuge publications as well as the supplies needed for various workshops held at the Center. In addition, some of the major exhibits were paid for by them, as were the interpretive panels on the wildlife drive. Matching funds were provided with a grant from the Fish and Wildlife Service to install a Travelers Information Radio Station accessible to traffic passing the Refuge on M-77.

In 1993 in recognition of its significant contribution to the Seney National Wildlife Refuge, the Seney Natural History Association was presented with the Outstanding Contribution Award from the U.S. Fish and Wildlife Service regional office.

*A Fishing Contest Prize Winner*  USFWS

*Seney National Wildlife Refuge Visitor Center* E. LOSEY

# VISITOR CENTER

rom its opening in 1965, the visitor center rapidly became the focal point for an ever increasing number of activities designed for visitor enjoyment and participation. The public responded enthusiastically and attendance steadily increased.

A host of special days and events were organized. The list was long. Included were outdoor classrooms stressing environmental education, teacher workshops, nature programs for school groups, field trips, weekly guided tours of the Refuge, fishing contests, photo contests, snow festivals, Scout Day, Endangered Species Day, Meet the Mammals Day, Love a Loon Day, National Hunting and Fishing Day, creating a float for local Fourth of July parades and presentation of wildlife films during the winter.

Public use of the Refuge continued to increase. The visitor center with its wildlife exhibits and display of wildlife books, tapes, posters and other related material attracted visitors in record numbers, reaching 88,000 in 1982. Commencing in 1982 the center was staffed by Retired Senior Citizen Volunteers, local residents over 60 years old. They assisted at the visitors center by answering questions at the information counter, showing wildlife movies and operating the bookstore. By the following year it

*Seney Refuge Float – 4th of July Parade* P. OVERHISER

*Cross Country Skiing at the Refuge*    USFWS

was evident that the services of these volunteers were essential if an adequate public use program for the visiting public was to be provided. In fact, by 1986 the successful operation of the visitor center had become nearly 100% dependent on the senior volunteers. The small handful of seniors which had first volunteered in 1982 had grown four years later to thirty-two.

The publication of the Refuge Reflections Newsletter was begun in 1991. This is an important source of information for the general public on Refuge activities, programs and current research projects. Published twice a year, it has wide distribution.

In recognition of their accomplishments, the Seney National Wildlife Volunteers were selected as state winners in the "Take Pride in America Program" for two successive years. They also received the Fish and Wildlife Service "Take Pride in America" award.

Recognizing the mounting importance of the Refuge public use programs, in 1990 a permanent full-time public use position was created to handle these new responsibilities and projects. Eleven years later it was necessary to add a second full-time seasonal post.

*Photographing the Trumpeters*    K. COUDRET

# TRACY CASSELMAN - REFUGE MANAGER
## 2001 - PRESENT

*I*n mid 2001 Tracy Casselman became the twelfth Seney Refuge Manager . He looks forward to building on the work and research already accomplished at the Refuge over the past years. In particular, he plans to establish and promote liaison not only with state and federal government agencies but also with non-government organizations that are involved with the administration of natural resources. He also wishes to build strong relations with the local community through participation in group events, so that the Refuge, its purposes and its program will become better known and understood.

The new manager favors increased use of fire as a management tool for creating areas in varying stages of forest succession to meet the needs of different species of wildlife. He also feels the need to establish fire breaks in certain areas as safeguards against potential fire hazards.

The practice of long term timber cutting to create, encourage, and maintain diverse types of woodland habitat will be continued and possibly expanded. Attention will be focused on those species in special need of help, such as the Yellow Rail, the Sharp-tailed Grouse, and many of the grassland birds such as the Bobolink and several species of sparrows.

Casselman admits that one of his major tasks will be to formulate a fifteen-year plan (as required by the Fish and Wildlife Service) to chart the future direction of the Refuge which will conform to the new Fish and Wildlife policy of making each Refuge a component link in the over-all ecosystem of the entire Refuge system.

# SENEY NATIONAL WILDLIFE REFUGE
## AN EVALUATION

Seney National Wildlife Refuge welcomes the 21st century. Much has been accomplished during the sixty-seven years since its beginning in 1935. The Refuge infrastructure is well established. The extensive system of roads, dikes and impoundments as well as the administrative and service buildings have all been built. Significant research into a wide range of biological subjects is ongoing with the results frequently being published in appropriate journals.

A modern visitor center has been built. Here the public finds interesting and informative exhibits of birds and mammals as well as a wide variety of natural history books, tapes and pictures. Most importantly, it is the center which sponsors numerous special wildlife oriented events for public participation. In short, the visitor center is fulfilling its chief function of providing the public with not only a pleasant experience but also a glimpse into the world of wildlife and conservation.

The future challenges and problems which face the Refuge are many. The need to balance, in an equitable way, the needs for continuing biological research and for marsh and forest improvement and rehabilitation against the ever expanding requirements of the resources devoted to visitor use, require careful, impartial and far-sighted decisions.

Seney Refuge is a safe haven for wildlife. It is a place where the solemn words "preserve, protect, and defend" apply not only to the people of the United States but also to the wildlife within Refuge borders.

It is a place where the public is encouraged to come to see and enjoy wildlife, to participate in wildlife-related activities and to gain an understanding of the vital role the Refuge plays in managing the wildlife entrusted to its care.

It is a place honoring and practicing Aldo Leopold's land ethic, an affirmation that wildlife in all its diverse forms – whether bird, mammal, fish, or plant – is entitled to be treated in an ethical and moral manner.

The Seney National Wildlife Refuge is ready and able to meet these challenges and responsibilities. It faces the 21st century with confidence.

# APPENDIX I

## SENEY NATIONAL WILDLIFE REFUGE MANAGERS

| | |
|---|---|
| C. S. Johnson | 1935-1949 |
| Cordia J. Henry | 1949-1958 |
| Edward J. Smith | 1958-1959 |
| Jerald J. Wilson | 1959-1962 |
| Charles A. Hughlett | 1962-1963 |
| John B. Hakala | 1963-1967 |
| John B. Wilbrecht | 1967-1973 |
| Lawrence G. Kline | 1973-1973 |
| John R. Frye | 1974-1981 |
| Donald N. Frickie | 1981-1988 |
| Michael G. Tansy | 1989-2001 |
| Tracy Casselman | 2001-Present |

*Yellow Lady Slipper*                    R. BAETSEN

# APPENDIX II

## MAJOR PUBLICATIONS RESULTING FROM RESEARCH AT THE SENEY NATIONAL WILDLIFE REFUGE

| | |
|---|---|
| Anderson, Stanley H. | Effects of the 1976 Seney National Wildlife Refuge Wildfire on Wildlife and Wildlife Habitat. *U.S. Dept. Interior, Fish & Wildlife Service. Resource Publication 146.* (1982) |
| Beard, Elizabeth B. (Losey). | The Importance of Beaver in Waterfowl Management at the Seney National Wildlife Refuge. *Journal of Wildlife Management,* Vol. 28, No. 3, pp 492-521. (1964) |
| ---------------------------- | Duck Brood Behavior at the Seney National Wildlife Refuge. *Journal of Wildlife Management,* Vol. 28, No. 4, pp 398-436. (1964) |
| Burkman, Margaret. | The Use of Prescribed Fire to Enhance Nesting Habitat for Yellow Rails at Seney National Wildlife Refuge. MS Thesis. Northern Michigan University, Marquette, Michigan. (1993) |
| Crozier, Gaea Elizabeth. | Using Local Patch and Landscape Variables to Model Bird Abundance in a Naturally Heterogeneous Landscape. MS Thesis. University of Minnesota. (1999) |
| East, Ben. | The Canada Goose Can Be Brought Back. *Outdoor Life* (Feb. 1950) |
| Evers, David C. | A Replicable Capture Method for Adult and Juvenile Common Loons on Their Nesting Lakes. *American Loon Conference Proceedings, Bar Harbor, Maine, Publication # 13.* Whitefish Point Bird Observatory, pp 214-219. |
| ---------------------------- | Population Ecology of the Common Loon at the Seney National Wildlife Refuge, Seney, Michigan. Results from the First Color-marked Breeding Population. *American Loon Conference Proceedings, Bar Harbor, Maine. Publication # 12.* Whitefish Point Bird Observatory, pp 202-212. (1992) |
| Evers, David C., Joseph D. Kaplan, Peter S. Reaman, James D. Paruk, Paul Phifer. | Demographic Characteristics of the Common Loon in the Upper Great Lakes. *Proceedings of Symposium of American Ornithologists' Union, 115th Meeting, University of Minnesota.* Minneapolis, Minnesota. (1997) |
| Faber, Raymond A. and Joseph J. Hickey. | Insecticides, PCB's and Mercury in Inland Aquatic Bird Eggs. Patuxent Wildlife Research Center. Laurel, Maryland, pp 1-16. (1971) |
| Field, Ronald J. | Winter Habits of the River Otter, *Lutra canadensis* in Michigan. Michigan Academician, Vol. 3, No. 1, pp 49-58. (1970) |
| ---------------------------- | A Comparison of the Activities of the River Otter *(Lutra canadensis)* in Two Types of Ecological Habitats. MS Thesis. Michigan State University, East Lansing, Michigan. (1970) |

| | |
|---|---|
| Fjetland, C. A. | Long Term Survival of Plastic Collars on Geese. Fourth Canada Goose Ecology Seminar, Kellogg Sanctuary, Battle Creek, Michigan. (1970) |
| Heinselman, Dr. M.L. | String Bogs and Other Patterned Organic Terrain Near Seney, Upper Michigan. *Ecology,* Vol. 46, Nos. 1, 2. (Winter, 1965) |
| Johnson, C. S. | Canada Goose Management, Seney National Wildlife Refuge. *Journal of Wildlife Management,* Vol. 11, No. 1, pp 21-24. (1947) |
| Kowalski, Kurt P. | Analysis of Wetland Plant Communities and Environmental Conditions. A Wetland Restoration Project in Seney National Wildlife Refuge. MS Thesis. Eastern Michigan University, Ypsilanti, Michigan. (2000) |
| Lagler, Karl F. | The Pike, *Esox lucius linnaeus,* in Relation to Waterfowl on the Seney National Wildlife Refuge, Michigan. *Journal of Wildlife Management,* Vol. 20, No 2, pp 114-124. (1956) |
| Lishman, William A., Tighe L. Teets, Joseph W. Duff, William J.L. Sladen, Gavin G. Shire, Kirk M. Goolsby, Wayne A. Bezner Kerr, Richard P. Urbanek. | A Reintroduction Technique for Migratory Birds - Leading Canada Geese and Isolation-reared Sandhill Cranes with Ultralight Aircraft. pp 96-104. (1996) |
| McMillen, Janet L. | Evaluation of the Seney National Wildlife Refuge as a Reintroduction Site for Whooping Cranes. United States Fish and Wildlife Service. |
| Palmer, S.F. and D.O. Trainer. | Serological Study of Some Infectious Diseases of Canada Geese. *Bulletin Wildlife Disease Association,* Vol. 5, pp 260-266. |
| ------------------------- | Serological Evidence of Newcastle Disease Virus in Canada Geese. *Avian Diseases,* Vol 14, No. 3, pp 494-502 |
| Sarvis, John E. | The Breeding Biology and Ecology of the Ring-necked Duck on Seney National Wildlife Refuge. Unpublished Thesis. Utah State University, Logan Utah. (1971) |
| Sherwood, Glen A. | Recent Modifications in Banding Equipment for Canada Geese. *Journal of Wildlife Management,* Vol. 29, No. 3, pp 640-643. (1965) |
| ------------------------- | Canada Geese of the Seney National Wildlife Refuge. United States Department of the Interior, 222 pp. (1965) |
| ------------------------- | Canada Geese of the Seney National Wildlife Refuge. Doctoral Thesis. Utah State University, Logan, Utah, 300 pp. (1966) |
| ------------------------- | Behavior of Family Groups of Canada Geese. Transactions of the 32nd North American Wildlife Conference, pp 340-355. (1967) |
| Skutek, Stan A. | Preliminary Investigations of Sandhill Crane Feather Analysis. MS Thesis. University of Wisconsin. (1980) |

Tarshis, I. Barry.

Collecting and Rearing Black Flies. *Annals of the Entomological Society of America,* Vol. 61, No 5, pp 1072-1083.

Tarshis, I Barry and William Neil.

Mass Movement of Black Fly Larvae on Silken Threads. Annals of the Entomological Society of America, Vol. 63, No. 2, pp 607-610. (1970)

Urbanek, Richard P.

Behavior and Survival of Captive-reared Juvenile Sandhill Cranes Introduced by Gentle Release into a Migratory Flock of Sandhill Cranes. Unpublished Report. Ohio Cooperative Fish & Wildlife Research Unit, Columbus, Ohio. (1990)

Urbanek, Richard P. and T.A. Bookhout.

Nesting of Greater Sandhill Cranes on Seney National Wildlife Refuge. Proceedings of North American Crane Workshop, pp 161-172. (1988, 1992)

-----------------------------

Development of an Isolation-rearing Gentle Release Procedure for Reintroducing Migratory Cranes. Proceedings of North American Crane Workshop, Vol 6, pp 120-130.

-----------------------------

Performance of Captive-reared Cranes Released into a Migration Route in Eastern North America. The Future of Cranes and Wetlands. Wild Bird Society. H. Higuche and J. Minton, eds. Tokyo, Japan. (1994)

Walcott, Charles, and David Evers.

Loon Vocal Tagging: An Evaluation of its Feasibility using a Banded Population of Loons. Loons: Old History and New Findings. Symposium of American Ornithologists' Union, University of Minnesota, Minneapolis, Minnesota. (1997)

Walcott, Charles, David Evers,

Individuality in "Yodel" Calls Recorded from a Banded Population of Common Loons, *Gavia immer.* Bioacoustics. The International Journal of Animal Sound and its Recording. (1999), Vol. 10, pp 101-114. (1999)

Wenrui, Duan.

Social and Reproductive Behavior of Isolation-reared Released Sandhill Cranes *(Grus canadensis).* MS Thesis. Ohio State University. (1994)

Wenrui, Duan, Theodore A. Bookhout, Richard P. Urbanek.

Home Range and Habitat Use by Isolation-reared Sandhill Cranes. Proceedings of Seventh North American Crane Workshop. North American Crane Working Group. Biloxi, Mississippi. (January 1996) pp 72-78. (1996)

Wilbrecht, J.E.

Status of Seney Goose Population. Fourth Canada Goose Ecology Seminar. Kellogg Sanctuary, Battle Creek, Michigan. (1970)

*Family of Canada Geese*

R. BAETSEN

# APPENDIX III

## (Excerpt from the account written by C. S. Johnson in the Narrative Report for 1945)

*These pages are furnished by request, but reluctantly. We would prefer to forget the whole thing.*

Up to May 12, 1944 events pursued the even tenor of their way at this station, even up to the bright noon of that day when a few employees of the Fish and Wildlife Service and a bunch of strangers classified as conscientious objectors sat down to a fine dinner of roast pork, mashed potatoes and rich brown gravy, combination salad, tender green peas, hot buns, a selection of two kinds of pie, and coffee. The proud cook beamed thru the spotless glitter of the kitchen as he watched his provender being stowed away. Administrative personnel, exuding good humor and determinedly exhibiting appropriate tolerance for all forms of religious belief, covertly sized up their new charges and made plans for using Joe Whoozis and Henry Whatcamacallit for this and that. Up to 12:35 P.M. of May 12, 1944 official life on this Seney Refuge was normal, if not fine.

Most everybody had by then licked up the last delicious morsel of pie, and convinced himself that Archie was one hell of a swell cook. It was about time for the speech of welcome.

At 12:35.52 the froth of sprightly, highly educated chit-chat was rudely silenced by the sound of clanking chains and a shattering voice declaiming "This is slavery!" It was Bishop, a veteran of 5 camps, putting on his act, the main features of which were a ball and chain and a string of "quotations," Bishop, with the traditional beard of the prophets and other stage effects consisting of a Bible, an ascetic face and a fanatical gleam in his eye.

In our innocence, we immediately concluded that Bishop was a screwball and as such eligible to the sanitarium some 26 miles away. Arrangements were made that very day to put the gentleman in his proper environment, but the idea was abandoned upon instructions from Washington. We learned later that Bishop was just a fair sample of the C. O. group and his act, and his objective in using it, was one of many which were characteristic of the type of objectors selected for the Germfask camp. Bishop was one of the 20 or 30 objectors who were later sent to Federal prison. Even there he carried on his crusade for something or other, starving himself for 86 days, obtaining bonded release for an appeal, jilting his bondsman and finally ending up in prison under a four year sentence. We no longer hear about Bishop, but his spirit must have infested the camp, for it got no better during his absence, and his disciples kept the place in constant ferment up to the day when the camp made the headlines.

Up to that inevitable climax every day at camp was a chapter in itself, with the objectors trying to break up the camp by every means available, including the stealing of mess equipment such as dishes, stove doors and lids, theft and destruction of food, sabotage of the water supply system, the sewage system; hiding or stealing of working equipment, – even putting broken glass in the garbage to the irritation of the poor pigs which might well have fattened on this by product for the American war effort. The objective of the administration in this contest was to hold on until new regulations could be written to cure the situation. The objectors purpose was to show that the set-up would not work and the only solution was to crash thru with discharges for all the dissenters in the camp.

The deadlocked situation existed up to the last few days of the camp's existence, when a few men were sent away for reclassification to the armed services, or failing to do so (and we don't know if any really were inducted) being sent to prison. During the 12 months of the camp's duration, personnel changes were many, for the various positions were hardly to be desired. Five cooks and five camp managers, in particular, were hired during that period. The camp director, the project superintendent, two foremen, the camp clerk and the mechanic stuck it thru. Four camp doctors had a go at the "sick list" and special medical boards also had their fingers on the pulse of the camp. Specialists, FBI agents, State Police, U. S. Department of Justice officials, parole officers representing the Federal prisons, writers of all kinds, representatives of anti-war groups, American Legion delegations, several U.S. Congressmen, inspectors of various Federal Agencies came – and went.

It can be truthfully said that the main activity of this camp was refusal to work.

*Skunk*                                                                                    R. DENOMME

# MAP OF
# SENEY NATIONAL WILDLIFE REFUGE

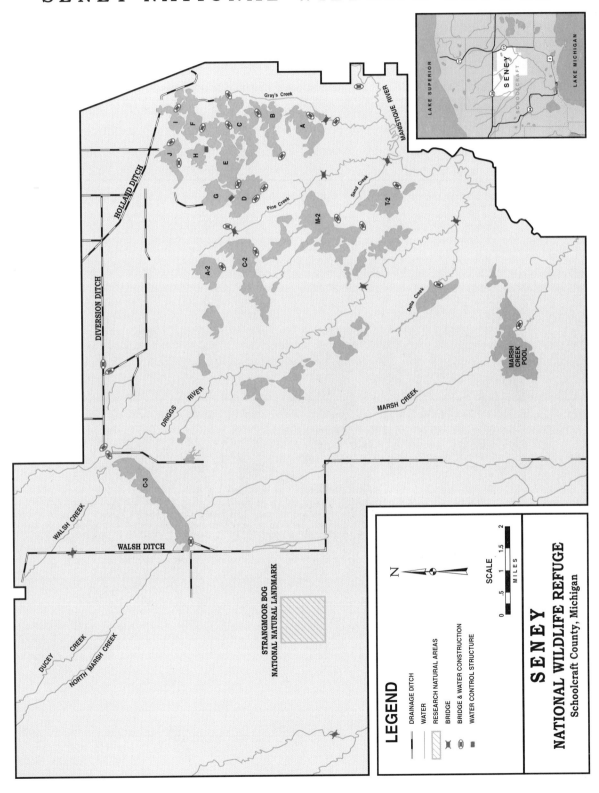

*Refuge Manager's Residence and Administrative Building*   C. HENRY

*Elizabeth B. Losey — Biologist, 1947*    DETROIT NEWS

Elizabeth Browne Losey is truly one of the unsung pioneers in the field of Wildlife Management. Although she worked only a few years in the profession, she has many firsts to her credit. Among them, she was the first female field biologist hired to work for the National Wildlife Refuge System and the first to be elected to active professional membership in the Wildlife Society in 1948.

She was born Elizabeth Browne in 1912 and grew up near Marblehead, Massachusetts. As a child, she developed a passion for the outdoors and learned to identify birds, as she calls it, "the lazy way" by listening to their songs. Elizabeth attended the University of Michigan, where she earned a B.A. in 1934 and a M.S. in 1946 majoring in the new field of Wildlife Management and Conservation. For several years she developed and taught courses in waterfowl and upland game bird management. After completing her studies, she was hired by J. Clark Salyer to conduct field work at Seney National Wildlife Refuge. Her work earned her the respect of the Refuge Manager and the wildlife profession. C.S. Johnson, Seney's first Refuge Manager, wrote of Mrs. Losey "...she is going to be heard from in wildlife circles..." His prediction rang true in 1954 when her paper entitled *The Importance of Beaver in Waterfowl Management at the Seney National Wildlife Refuge* published in the Journal of Wildlife Management received Honorable Mention in the Wildlife's Society's annual North American 1954 competition.

Although she did not stay in the field of conservation, Elizabeth Losey never lost her passion for wildlife and when I met her a year ago I was as impressed as C.S. Johnson was in 1947. Her skill at research and dedication to writing this book are admirable. She worked daily reading annual narratives, reviewing records and compiling text and then taught herself to use a computerized word processing program despite her aging hands and eyes. Elizabeth Losey is a remarkable woman who will once again be heard from in wildlife circles.

–Tracy Casselman, *Refuge Manager*

*Sandhill Crane Chick*                                        J. REUTHER

# ACKNOWLEDGMENTS

Especial gratitude to Rick Baetsen of Northwind Photography, Rick Denomme's Natural Image, Ted and Jean Reuther, and Karl Sommerer for generously donating so many of their splendid wildlife photographs.

Thanks to the Seney National Wildlife Refuge for granting permission to use its files and photographs.

Sincere appreciation to the Seney Natural History Association for financing publication costs.

The author is indebted to T. Casselman, M. Tansy and M. Kronk for helpful suggestions and a critical review of the text.